BENBROOK PUBLIC LIBRARY

3426700109093О

D1469935

Benbrook Public Library

IT'S COOL TO LEARN ABOUT COUNTRIES

Social Studies Explorer

VIETNAM

✦ by Dana Meachen Rau

CHERRY LAKE PUBLISHING • ANN ARBOR, MICHIGAN

Published in the United States of America
by Cherry Lake Publishing
Ann Arbor, Michigan
www.cherrylakepublishing.com

Content Adviser: Charles Keith, PhD, Department of History,
Michigan State University, East Lansing, Michigan

The author would like to thank Janet Lawler and Kim Nguyen for reviewing this
manuscript and sharing their expertise.

Book design: The Design Lab

Photo credits: Cover, ©Rafal Cichawa/Shutterstock, Inc. and ©iStockphoto.com/
AlexanderZam; page 4, ©Eddy Van Ryckeghem/Dreamstime.com; page 6, ©Cyril Hou/
Shutterstock, Inc.; page 8, ©Bzzuspajk/Shutterstock, Inc.; page 9, ©dean bertoncelj/
Shutterstock, Inc.; page 10, ©Scubabartek/Dreamstime.com; page 12, ©beboy/Shutterstock,
Inc.; page 14, ©Anibal Trejo/Shutterstock, Inc.; page 15, ©Marilo Bertomeu/Shutterstock,
Inc.; page 17, ©imagebroker/Alamy; page 18, ©ITAR-TASS Photo Agency/Alamy; page 19,
©Fotogroove/Shutterstock, Inc.; page 20, ©Piero Cruciatti/Dreamstime.com; page 21, ©Paul
Thompson Images/Alamy; page 22, ©zeber/Shutterstock, Inc.; page 25, ©Juha Sompinmäki/
Shutterstock, Inc.; page 26, ©Valery Shanin/Shutterstock, Inc.; page 27, ©Hans Kemp/
Alamy; page 29, ©David R. Frazier Photolibrary, Inc./Alamy; page 30, ©Skip Nall/Alamy;
pages 34 and 40, ©Nigel Spiers/Dreamstime.com; page 35, ©Supereagle/Dreamstime.com;
page 36, ©Kumikomurakamicampos/Dreamstime.com; page 39, ©Margouillat/Dreamstime.
com; page 42, ©Louise Rivard/Dreamstime.com; page 43, ©Josef Muellek/Dreamstime.com;
page 44, ©Koon Hong Kang/Dreamstime.com; page 45, ©Stephen Lloyd Vietnam/Alamy

Copyright ©2012 by Cherry Lake Publishing
All rights reserved. No part of this book may be reproduced or utilized in
any form or by any means without written permission from the publisher.

Library of Congress Cataloging-in-Publication Data
Rau, Dana Meachen, 1971–
  It's cool to learn about countries. Vietnam/by Dana Meachen Rau.
    p. cm.—(Social studies explorer)
  Includes index.
  ISBN-13: 978-1-61080-097-6 (library binding)
  ISBN-10: 1-61080-097-4 (library binding)
  1. Vietnam—Juvenile literature. I. Title. II. Title: Vietnam.
  DS556.3.R38 2012
  959.7—dc22   2010053751

Cherry Lake Publishing would like to acknowledge the work of The Partnership for
21st Century Skills. Please visit www.21stcenturyskills.org for more information.

Printed in the United States of America
Corporate Graphics Inc.
July 2011
CLFA09

TABLE OF CONTENTS

IBIS LEUCOCEPHALUS_CÔ LAO

CHAPTER ONE
WELCOME TO VIETNAM!

◄► Water buffalo are important to Vietnamese farmers.

If you look at a globe, it is easy to spot Asia. It is the largest continent in terms of land. It is also the continent with the most people. The combined population of Asia's many countries is in the billions! Let's stop in one of these countries—Vietnam—to explore life on the other side of the world.

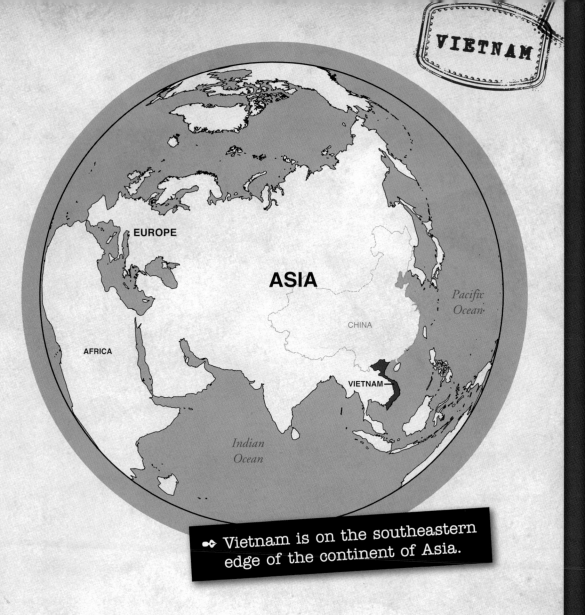

EUROPE

ASIA

CHINA

Pacific Ocean

AFRICA

VIETNAM

Indian Ocean

◆ Vietnam is on the southeastern edge of the continent of Asia.

Vietnam is long and skinny. It is tucked along the southeastern edge of Asia, next to the Gulf of Tonkin and the South China Sea. Laos and Cambodia border it to the west, and China borders it to the north. Vietnam's total area is about 128,000 square miles (332,000 square kilometers), making it a little larger than the state of New Mexico. Almost 90 million people live in Vietnam.

➥ Rice fields often fill the valleys of northern Vietnam.

Wider at the top and bottom, and skinny in the middle, Vietnam has three regions: Bac Bo (northern), Trung Bo (central), and Nam Bo (southern). The landscape of the north contains mountains, hills, and plains. Fan Si Pan, the country's highest peak, stands in the north. The Red River and other waterways cross this area. Crops such as rice grow in the **fertile** plains along these rivers. This region is also home to Hanoi, the country's capital.

The Truong Son Mountains run down the western edge of central Vietnam. But on the eastern side, you'll find the beaches and harbors of the coast. The central region gets some of the worst weather. Swirling storms with high winds called **typhoons** often crash into the shore.

Vietnam is one of the world's narrowest countries. Central Vietnam is only 30 miles (48 km) across at its narrowest point. If a freeway crossed the country at this point, a car could drive from one side to the other in less than a half hour.

To the other side

IBIS LEUCOCEPHALUS_CỐ LAO

Boats are a common site along the Mekong River.

The Mekong River is an important waterway running through southern Vietnam. Sometimes it is called the River of Nine Dragons because it splits into nine smaller rivers before it empties into the South China Sea. The land around this wide **delta** is rich for farming. The country's largest city, Ho Chi Minh City (formerly called Saigon), lies in the south.

From the rugged mountains to the sunny beaches, Vietnam has breathtaking views of nature. In Ha Long

Bay, more than 3,000 islands rise up from the water. Legend says that the islands formed when a dragon dropped jewels and jade into the clear bay.

Vietnam has a tropical climate, meaning it is typically warm and wet. The northern part of the country has four seasons. Summers are hot and humid, with

Vietnam's land provides homes for many animals. Creatures live in the rugged mountains, the thick forests, the rushing rivers, and on the salty coast. Vietnam's magnificent wildlife includes the Sarus crane, the clouded leopard, the water buffalo, and the endangered Javan rhinoceros.

temperatures often rising above 90 degrees Fahrenheit (32 degrees Celsius). Winters are much drier and cooler. The south has only two seasons. The rainy season runs from May to September. The dry season runs from October through April. Throughout the year, the high temperature in the south hovers around 90°F (32°C). In both the north and the south, the climate is much milder in the mountains. All across the country, **monsoon** winds blow in from the southwest during summer and early fall, often bringing heavy rain.

Monsoons can result in floods across Vietnam.

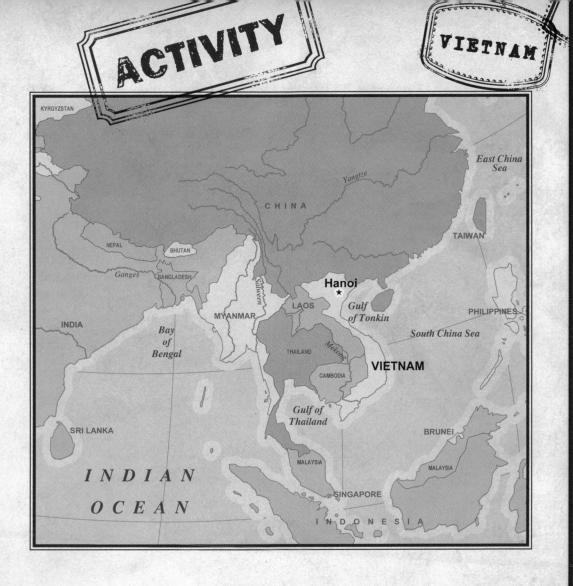

Rivers flow downhill, from high areas to low areas, until they eventually flow into the ocean. Many rivers start in one country and end in another. Place a piece of paper over the map above and trace the route of the Mekong River. Find its start in China. Then follow its route through Laos, Cambodia, and Vietnam until you reach the ocean. Why do you think people first settled along rivers? How might rivers have helped them travel, farm, and survive?

CHAPTER TWO

BUSINESS AND GOVERNMENT IN VIETNAM

➥ A rice farmer picks rice on a rice paddy.

In Ho Chi Minh City, a businessman talks on a cell phone while riding his motorbike. In the country, a woman wearing a large woven hat stoops in a rice paddy, or field. All over Vietnam, people work to make a living.

A rice paddy is a flooded field of land. Farmers bend over the rice to plant and harvest. They use water buffalo for heavy work, like plowing. The farmers wear cone-shaped hats called *non la* to protect themselves from the sun and keep cool.

Vietnam is a Communist country, one in which the government controls the economy. In the past, the government controlled all of Vietnam's business. But in recent years, the government has established new policies that have helped the economy grow. Vietnam's economy now includes private businesses and more trade with other countries. Large cargo ships leave the country's ports to bring products to the United States, Japan, China, Europe, Australia, and many other trading partners. Tourism has also become a major industry in Vietnam in recent years. About 4 million foreign visitors travel to Vietnam every year.

Vietnam's currency is called the dong. Paper money, or banknotes, range from 200 dong to 500,000 dong. All banknotes have a picture of Ho Chi Minh, an important 20th-century political leader. Coins, which were introduced in 2004, come in amounts ranging from 200 dong to 5,000 dong. In 2011, one U.S. dollar equaled nearly 21,000 dong.

Most Vietnamese people are farmers. Their largest crop is rice. In fact, Vietnam is the second-largest **exporter** of rice in the world. Farmers grow the most rice in the Mekong and Red River Deltas. Besides rice, farmers also grow black pepper, coffee, and tea. Other crops grown in Vietnam include cashews, peanuts,

sugarcane, sweet potatoes, and cotton. Fruit crops include bananas, oranges, and coconuts.

Farmers also raise pork and poultry. Vietnamese fishers harvest fish and other seafood from the coast. Vietnam has a huge shrimp industry. The country is the second-largest shrimp exporter in the world. In 2010, Vietnam sold $2 billion worth of shrimp to other countries.

◆ Vietnamese fishers cast nets to pull in fish.

Percentages show how common something is, based on a total number of 100. (For example, 50 percent means 50 out of 100.) Based on the percentages on the pie chart, which grouping of stick figures represents the number of people involved in agriculture? Which group represents those in industry? Which group represents the number of people who work in services?

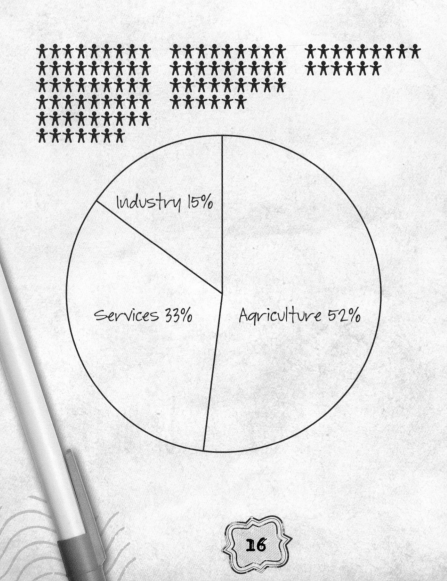

Forestry is another important industry in Vietnam. Trees provide rubber and timber. The mining industry processes coal, oil, zinc, copper, and silver. Some Vietnamese people work in factories making **textiles**, shoes, machines, paper, building materials, and other products. Service workers work in hotels and restaurants, do repairs, and sell goods in stores and malls.

The official name of Vietnam is the Socialist Republic of Vietnam. Its most recent **constitution**, which dates

❖ Vietnam has been producing silk for thousands of years.

➤ Vietnamese president Nguyen Minh Triet (left) shakes hands with Dmitry Medvedev, the president of Russia.

back to 1992, states that the Communist Party runs the country. The National Assembly is in charge of making laws and overseeing the economy. The National Assembly elects the president and the prime minister. The president's job is to represent the country. The prime minister is in charge of the daily workings of the government. His cabinet of **ministers** reports to him on different areas, including transportation, trade, health, and education. The National Assembly also elects the head of the

Supreme People's Court. This court helps make sure people and the government uphold the laws.

Vietnam is broken up into 58 provinces and 5 municipalities, each with its own smaller government. People elect leaders to their local People's Council, which is in charge of making laws for that area. The council then elects members to be on a People's Committee to represent the region.

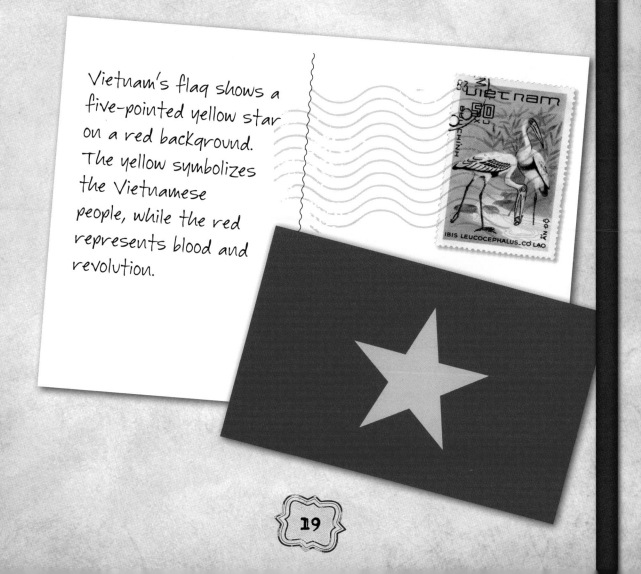

Vietnam's flag shows a five-pointed yellow star on a red background. The yellow symbolizes the Vietnamese people, while the red represents blood and revolution.

CHAPTER THREE

MEET THE PEOPLE

➥ A woman carries her baby on her back in Sapa in northern Vietnam.

The first Vietnamese people settled around the Red River about 5,000 years ago. Vietnam's history is filled with battles and disagreements as control of the area passed from China to Vietnam to France to Japan. Eventually, in 1945, Vietnam became an independent country under Ho Chi Minh, the leader of the Vietnamese Communist

Party. In the 1940s, a civil war broke out in Vietnam over which form of government was best for Vietnam. Many Vietnamese call it the American War because U.S. involvement made the war longer and more destructive. The war lasted until 1975, when the whole country came under Communist rule.

Today, Ho Chi Minh City and Hanoi are the two largest cities in Vietnam. In 2009 about 7.2 million people lived in Ho Chi Minh City and 6.5 million lived in Hanoi. But most Vietnamese live in the countryside, along the Red River and Mekong River Deltas.

Motorbikes are a popular form of transportation on crowded city streets.

In delta villages, some families live in houses on stilts in case the rivers flood. Some live in houses that float right on the water. Villagers shop at floating markets, paddling their flat-bottomed wooden boats, called sampans, to trade and buy goods. Homes in coastal, country, or mountain areas may be made of wood, clay, brick, or woven bamboo. In cities many families crowd into apartment buildings. People ride bikes or motorbikes through thickly crowded streets.

➥ Homes float in Halong Bay at the base of the cliffs.

VIETNAMESE

Vietnamese is the official language of Vietnam. It is a tonal language, which means that one word can have six different meanings. Tone is the way your voice rises or lowers at the beginning or end of a word, and how high or low you say it. The list of words below is a common example of how a change in tone can change meanings. The same two letters mean very different things, depending on how you say them. The accent marks tell you how to pronounce the word. Practice these words by changing your tone.

ENGLISH	VIETNAMESE
Mother	Má (rising high tone)
Horse	Mã (low tone to high tone with a break in between)
Ghost	Ma (flat, level tone)
Rice seedling	Mạ (falling low tone that you cut off sharply)
But/that	Mà (falling low tone)
Tomb	Mà (falling low tone, rising gently back up to a high tone)

In the country and city, children go to school. By law all children must go to school for 9 years. Just like kids in other parts of the world, they take breaks from class for recess and stay up late doing homework. Students have the option of attending high school for 3 years. Many then go on to colleges and universities.

Vietnam is home to 54 different ethnic groups. The largest, called the Viet or Kinh, includes more than 85 percent of the population. The Viet live mainly in the delta areas and the plains near the coast. Other ethnic groups include the Tay, Thai, Muong, Khmer, Hoa, Nun, and Hmong.

The traditional dress of Vietnam is the ao dai. This style includes loose pants worn under a shirt with side slits. Fancy versions are worn for special occasions. Simpler versions are sometimes worn as school or work uniforms. Sometimes a traditional style of dress identifies a person's ethnic group. The Red Dao are known for bright red turbans. The Flower Hmong wear layered outfits of colorful cloth.

IBIS LEUCOCEPHALUS_CÒ LÀO

→ Incense can be burned safely in incense vases.

Vietnam does not have an official religion, but people worship in many different ways. Families worship their **ancestors**. To honor these past relatives, they make offerings of flowers, food, and **incense** at family altars or public **pagodas**. Many people believe their ancestors protect them.

Over time, other religious traditions have also taken hold in Vietnam. Many Vietnamese follow Mahayana Buddhism combined with Confucianism and Taoism. This faith is called Tam Giao, or Three Religions. Catholicism is also common. Visitors and settlers from Portugal, Spain, and France brought Catholicism to Vietnam. Hoa Hao and Cao Dai are religions practiced only in Vietnam and neighboring Cambodia.

⟝ Worshippers fill the Cao Dai Temple in southern Vietnam.

CHAPTER FOUR

CELEBRATIONS!

❖ People of all ages look forward to Tet each year!

Chúc mùng năm mói—Happy New Year!

New Year's is the biggest celebration of the year in Vietnam. It is called Tet, which is short for

Tet Nguyen Dan. Tet can fall in January or February because the Vietnamese follow the lunar calendar, one based on the movements of the moon. Tet marks the beginning of the lunar calendar year.

Many Vietnamese believe that kitchen spirits protect their family. The week before Tet, families send these spirits on a journey to visit the Jade Emperor in heaven. They put out a tall bamboo pole decorated with small pieces of clay. In the breeze, the clay chimes and scares away evil spirits. On New Year's Eve, people celebrate

Tet is everyone's birthday. Vietnamese people don't celebrate birthdays on the day that they were born. When a child is born, he or she is already considered 1 year old. On Tet the child turns a year older.

➥ Drummers perform for a crowd of celebrators in Ho Chi Minh City.

with noisy drums, gongs, and fireworks to welcome the kitchen spirits back and to scare away unlucky ones. The Vietnamese celebrate Tet with feasts, parades, friends, and family.

Some Vietnamese visit cemeteries at Tet to invite their dead relatives to join in the celebrations. They clean and fix their homes, decorate with kumquat trees and peach blossoms, and buy new clothes. Tet is also a time to pray for good luck. Adults give children red envelopes of lucky money called *li xi*. Families also believe that the first visitor to their home in the new year will determine their own luck for the year to come. They try to invite a successful, lucky person.

❧ Lucky money envelopes are hung as decorations from kumquat trees.

A unique type of puppetry called *roi nuoc* has a long tradition in Vietnam. Puppeteers stand waist-deep in water with a curtain in front of them. They use underwater rods to make puppets perform on the stage of water. The puppets act out folktales and historical stories.

A roi nuoc puppet ↓

Another popular holiday, especially for children, is Trung Thu. Cities and villages are abuzz with music, singing, and dancing. Children eat moon cake treats and listen to traditional stories. They parade through the streets with lanterns shaped like stars, moons, fish, butterflies, and dragons.

MAKE A LANTERN!

For the holiday of Trung Thu, children parade in the streets with lanterns. Make your own lantern to celebrate!

MATERIALS

- Pencil
- 2 pieces of vellum paper, a stiff paper found at craft stores
- Scissors
- Hole puncher
- Yarn
- Glow stick or small flashlight
- Wooden dowel

INSTRUCTIONS

1. With a pencil, draw a star shape on a piece of vellum paper. Cut it out with scissors. Trace this star onto the other piece of paper and cut it out. Now you have two stars of the same size.

2. Fold each star in half along one of the points and then unfold. Then fold it in half again at each point, for a total of five times. (Your stars will have 10 lines coming out from the center.)

3. Place the two stars together, so they are perfectly lined up. Punch evenly spaced holes around the edges.

4. Separate the stars, and refold the creases so that the longer creases (the ones at each point) fold out, like a mountain, and the shorter creases fold in like a valley. Your stars will be three-dimensional.

5. Place the stars together again, lined up at the holes. Thread yarn through the hole at the top of one point, going through both stars. Leave about a 12-inch (30 centimeter) tail. Sew the yarn over and under through the holes around the outside of the stars.

6. Before you get back to the top, tie a glow stick or small flashlight to the yarn and let it hang down into the star. Finish sewing up to the top point.

7. Tie the two ends of the yarn together to keep it secure. Then tie the ends to a wooden dowel. Now you have a lantern!

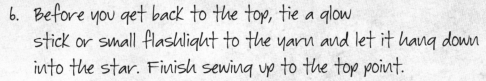

➥ A board game called Xianqi, also known as Chinese Chess, is popular in Vietnam.

Soccer is one of the most popular sports in Vietnam. People enjoy both watching it and playing it. Vietnamese people also like gymnastics and net sports, such as table tennis, volleyball, and badminton. Many people practice martial arts and play chess.

CHAPTER FIVE

WHAT'S FOR DINNER?

➥ Rice is a part of most meals.

Rice is the main crop grown in Vietnam, so it's no surprise that it's also the main ingredient in most meals. People serve rice as a side dish. They also use it to make rice noodles, rice wine, rice vinegar, rice paper, and sweetened rice cakes.

The Vietnamese use rice noodles in a soup called *pho*, which is sometimes considered the country's national dish. They place noodles and strips of beef or chicken in the bottom of a bowl, and pour hot spicy broth over them. They top the soup with fresh herbs. Pho is eaten any time of day, including at breakfast.

➥ Pho and other dishes are usually eaten with chopsticks.

Pho bo is a soup made with beef broth, rice noodles, and fresh herbs and spices. You'll need to use a hot stove and a sharp knife, so ask for an adult's help to make this simple variation of a traditional dish. This recipe makes four servings.

Pho Bo

INGREDIENTS
4 cups (1 liter) canned beef broth
1 package of rice noodles
4 green onions
$\frac{1}{4}$ pound (110 grams) deli roast beef
1 large handful mung bean sprouts
1 red chili pepper, sliced

Basil leaves
Cilantro leaves
Lime juice

INSTRUCTIONS

1. Pour the broth into a saucepan. Bring to a boil over high heat. Then reduce the heat, cover, and let simmer for 10 minutes.
2. Meanwhile, in a separate pan, cook the rice noodles according to package directions. Drain the water.
3. Slice the onions into small rings. Slice the roast beef into thin strips.
4. Take out 4 soup bowls. Place a serving size of cooked noodles in each bowl. Add a few strips of roast beef on top. Sprinkle the onions into each bowl.
5. Ladle about 1 cup of boiling hot broth into each bowl.
6. Top each with bean sprouts, chili pepper, basil, cilantro, and a squirt of lime juice.

Enjoy!

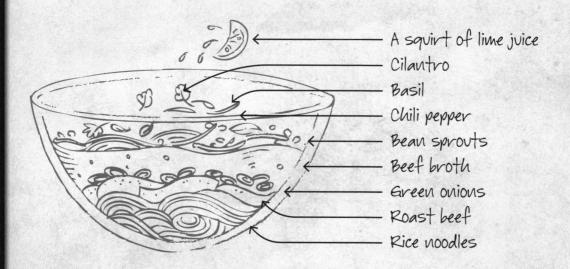

- A squirt of lime juice
- Cilantro
- Basil
- Chili pepper
- Bean sprouts
- Beef broth
- Green onions
- Roast beef
- Rice noodles

Flat rice paper is used to wrap finely chopped ingredients into a roll shape. These rolls are filled with meat and vegetables, such as pork, crab, onions, and mushrooms. The rolls are steamed or fried into crispy snacks.

Rice is sweetened using coconut milk. *Banh chung*, a traditional Tet treat, is a cake of sweetened rice, mung beans, and pork. People tie up the cake in banana leaves so it looks like a gift.

➥ These rice paper rolls are called spring rolls.

Vietnam's long coastline provides a lot of seafood! The Vietnamese eat crabs, prawns, shrimp, and fish. They also eat pork, beef, and poultry. Some eat meats that are not often eaten in the United States, such as snake, frog, and bat.

→ Vendors sell a variety of meal ingredients, such as vegetables, spices, and even chickens.

Some food traditions in Vietnam come from other cultures. They typically use chopsticks to eat their food. This habit came from the Chinese. From the French, the Vietnamese learned to enjoy crusty breads called baguettes. Vietnamese people often eat baguettes for breakfast.

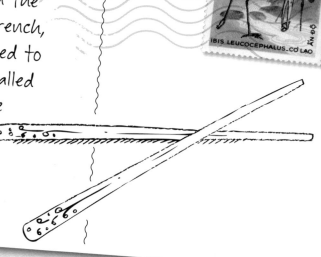

Families and restaurants serve raw vegetables as a side dish with meals. Cooks like to add pickled vegetables, such as eggplant or radish. *Rau muong*, or water spinach, is used in stir-fries and soups.

Vietnamese people add flavor to their food with lemongrass, basil, cilantro, ginger, peanuts, coconut milk, and mint. One of the most important ingredients is a fish sauce called *nuoc mam*. It's made by layering salt and fish in barrels and letting it sit for up to a year. Just like you might have salt on the table, Vietnamese

➬ This market in the southern Vietnam village of An Thoi is full of colorful fruit choices.

kitchens and restaurants have bottles of nuoc mam or *nuoc cham*, which is nuoc mam mixed with chilis, lime, vinegar, sugar, and garlic.

Many fruits, such as bananas, coconuts, **durians**, **rambutans**, and pomelos, grow well in Vietnam's warm, wet climate. Popular drinks include tea, coffee, fruit juice, soft drinks, and refreshing coconut milk.

At dinner a Vietnamese family places bowls of food on the table. Each person takes a serving of rice and then adds meat, fish, or vegetables on top. It's good table manners to bring the bowl close to your mouth. That way you don't have to lift your food too far and perhaps drop it off your chopsticks!

Markets floating in the water or crowded along city streets sell everything from fish and meat to vegetables and fruit. Few households in the country have refrigerators, so the Vietnamese shop at markets for fresh food every few days.

IBIS LEUCOCEPHALUS-CÒ LAO

Families aren't always home for meals. In cities and villages, street vendors set up stalls where customers can get a quick bite. Some vendors carry baskets with all the ingredients and utensils to make a customer a hot meal right on the spot. Pushcarts sell bowls of pho, spring rolls, or sweet snacks. Sweet treats might be rice cookies, fried bananas, or coconut candy. During Tet, children enjoy sugared dried fruit called *mut* and dried watermelon seeds.

❧ A vendor might carry goods in baskets on his or her shoulders, or on a bicycle.

◆ Students sit on a rickshaw in Ho Chi Minh City.

From north to south, mountains to coast, Vietnam has an amazing variety of people and places to discover. On a visit, you'll try new foods, explore the bustling cities, and enjoy the rich beauty of the country. Let's go!

GLOSSARY

ancestors (AN-sess-turz) people from whom one is descended

constitution (kon-stih-TOO-shuhn) a document that sets up a government system

delta (DEL-tuh) area of land made by deposits of mud or sand where a river spreads out or overflows

durians (DUR-ee-uhnz) large, oval fruits with prickly rinds

exporter (EK-sport-er) a country that sends a product to another country to be sold there

fertile (FUR-tuhl) capable of supporting rich plant growth

incense (IN-sens) a stick that lets off a pleasing smell when burned

ministers (MIN-ih-sturz) the heads of certain departments in a government

monsoon (mahn-SOON) seasonal winds

pagodas (puh-GOH-duhs) buildings with curved roofs used as places of worship or reflection

rambutans (ram-BOO-tenz) bright red, spiny fruits

textiles (TEK-stylz) fabrics made by knitting or weaving

typhoons (tye-FOONZ) swirling storms that form over tropical waters

Books

Green, Jen. *Vietnam.* Washington, DC: National Geographic, 2008.

O'Connor, Karen. *Vietnam.* Minneapolis: Lerner, 2009.

Web Sites

Learn About Vietnam
www.vietnamembassy-usa.org/learn_about_vietnam/
This official site of the Embassy of Vietnam is filled with facts about the people, government, economy, and culture of the country.

National Geographic Kids: Vietnam
http://kids.nationalgeographic.com/kids/places/find/vietnam/
Find facts, photos, videos, and maps of Vietnam at this site.

Time for Kids: Vietnam
www.timeforkids.com/TFK/kids/hh/goplaces
Visit countries around the world with these sightseeing guides. Click on Vietnam to take a tour of its places and people.

ABOUT THE AUTHOR
Dana Meachen Rau loves to discover something new about the world every day. She has written more than 250 books for children and lives with her family in Burlington, Connecticut.